KU-132-446

Creature Comparisons

Fish

Tracey Crawford

www.heinemann.co.uk/library
Visit our website to find out more information about **Heinemann Library** books.

To order:
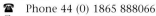 Phone 44 (0) 1865 888066
Send a fax to 44 (0) 1865 314091
Visit the Heinemann Bookshop at www.heinemann.co.uk/library to browse our
catalogue and order online.

First published in Great Britain by Heinemann Library, Halley Court, Jordan Hill, Oxford OX2 8EJ, part of Harcourt Education. Heinemann is a registered trademark of Harcourt Education Ltd.

© Harcourt Education Ltd 2007.
The moral right of the proprietor has been asserted.

Editorial: Tracey Crawford, Cassie Mayer, Dan Nunn, and Sarah Chappelow
Design: Jo Hinton-Malivoire
Picture Research: Tracy Cummins, Heather Mauldin, and Ruth Blair
Production: Duncan Gilbert

Originated by Chroma Graphics (Overseas) Pte. Ltd
Printed and bound in China by South China Printing Company

10 digit ISBN 0 431 18224 8
13 digit ISBN 978 0 431 18224 7

11 10 09 08 07
10 9 8 7 6 5 4 3 2 1

British Library Cataloguing in Publication Data
Crawford, Tracey
    Fish. - (Creature comparisons)
    1.Fishes - Juvenile literature
    I.Title
    597
A full catalogue record for this book is available from the British Library.

Acknowledgements
The publishers would like to thank the following for permission to reproduce photographs: Corbis pp. **4** (monkey, Frank Lukasseck/zefa; bird, Arthur Morris), **6** (Stephen Frink), **7** (Jeffrey L. Rotman), **9** (Royalty Free), **10** (Martin Harvey), **11** (Kit Kittle), **12** (Anthony Bannister), **14** (Louie Psihoyos), **15** (Stephen Frink), **16** (Brandon D. Cole), **18**, **19** (Amos Nachoum), **21** (Hal Beral), **22** (shark, Denis Scott; flounder, Brandon D. Cole), **23** (goldfish, Martin Harvey; Indo-Pacific Bluetang, Jeffrey L. Rotman; gray angelfish, Royalty Free); Getty Images pp. **5**, **17** (Hunt), **20** (Westmorland); Marinethemes.com p. **22** (hand fish, Kelvin Aitkenn); Naturepl.com p. **13** (Doug Perrine); Carlton Ward p. **4** (snake, frog).

Cover photograph of a blue tang reproduced with permission of Getty Images/Mike Kelly and a white spotted pufferfish reproduced with permission of Getty Images/Steven Hunt. Back cover photograph of an Indo-Pacific bluetang reproduced with permission of Corbis/Jeffrey L. Rotman.

Every effort has been made to contact copyright holders of any material reproduced in this book. Any omissions will be rectified in subsequent printings if notice is given to the publishers.

Contents

There are many types of animals.

Fish are one type of animal.

All fish live in water.

gill

All fish have gills.

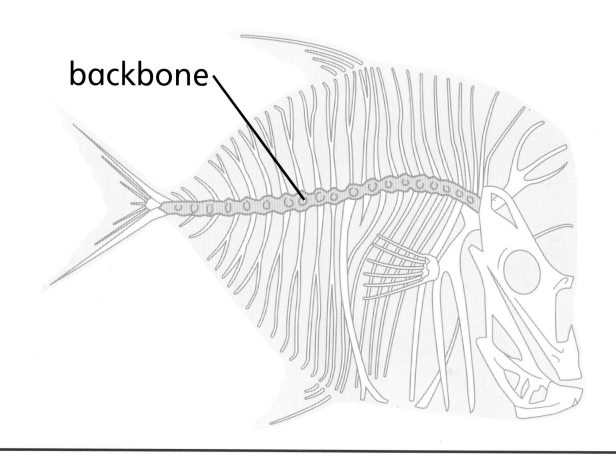

backbone

All fish have a backbone.

fin

tail

All fish have fins and a tail.

scales

Most fish have scales.

But this fish does not.

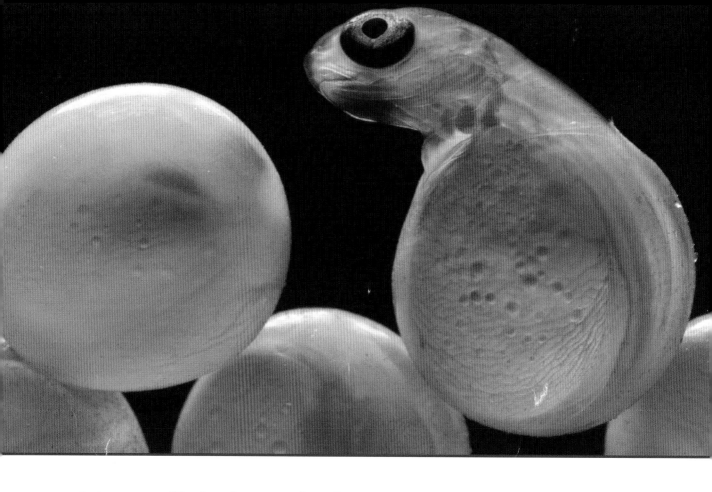

Most fish hatch from an egg.

baby shark

But this fish does not.

Some fish are big.

Some fish are small.

Some fish are flat.

Some fish are round.

Some fish hunt.

Some fish hide.

Every fish is different.

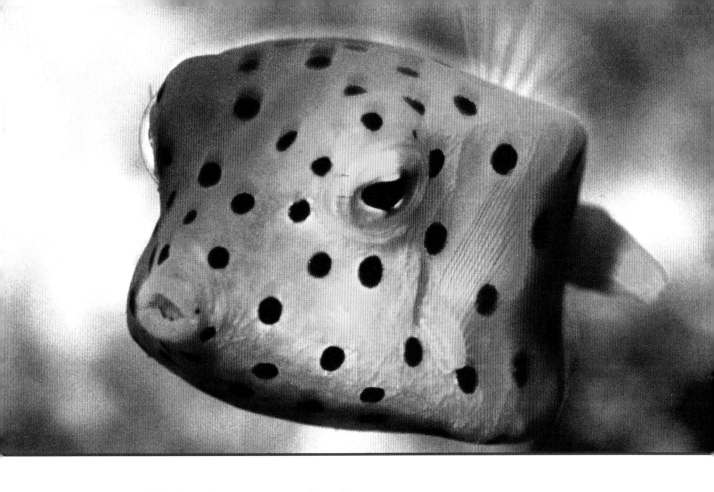

Every fish is special.

Fish facts

Sharks have many rows of teeth.

Flounders live on the ocean floor. They can change colour. This helps them hide.

Hand fish have fins that are like hands. These fish walk on the ocean floor.

Picture glossary

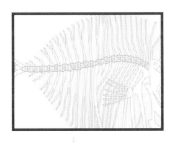 **backbone** the part of the skeleton that goes from the tail to the head

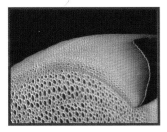 **fin** the part of a fish that helps it move through water

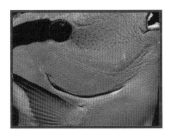 **gill** the part of a fish that helps it breathe

 **scale** a small, flat plate on the outside of an animal. Scales cover skin.

Index

Notes to parents and teachers
Before reading
Talk to the children about fish. Does anyone keep a pet fish? What different fish can they name?

After reading
Sing the nursery rhyme with hand actions: "One, two, three, four, five. Once I caught a fish alive. Six, seven, eight, nine, ten. Then I let it go again. Why did you let it go? Because it bit my finger so. Which finger did it bite? This little finger on the right."
Talk to the children about how fish move: They dart and jump and stand still and quiver. Tell them to use their hands to represent quivering gills. Play a recording of "The Trout" by Schubert and ask the children to move like fish in time to the music.
Tell the children to draw around their hand with the fingers splayed on to pieces of coloured card. Cut out and turn sideways. Add a google eye on the thumb pad and a mouth below. Arrange the fish swimming in the same direction on a large piece of blue card. Hang strips of green tissue paper to represent sea-weed and fronds.

Titles in the *Creature Comparisons* series include:

Hardback   0 431 18226 4

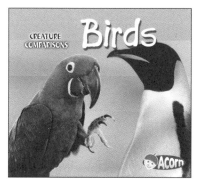

Hardback   0 431 18225 6

Hardback   0 431 18224 8

Hardback   0 431 18228 0

Hardback   0 431 18223 X

Hardback   0 431 18227 2

Find out about other titles from Heinemann Library on our website www.heinemann.co.uk/library